Book design by Theresa M. Sparacio.

Illustrations by Nicholas Markell

Copyright © 1993 by Daniel J. Porter

Library of Congress Cataloging-in-Publication Data

Porter, Daniel J., 1961-
    50 familiar sayings from the Bible/Daniel J. Porter.
        p.   cm.
    ISBN 0-8091-3422-5 (pbk.)
    1. Bible—Quotations. I. Title. II. Title: Fifty familiar sayings from the Bible.
BS391.2.P64   1993
242'.5—dc20   93-6012
                                                                  CIP

Published by Paulist Press
997 Macarthur Boulevard
Mahwah, New Jersey 07430

Printed and bound in the United States of America

50 FAMILIAR SAYINGS FROM THE BIBLE

DEDICATION

For my parents, Tom and Trudy,
for their love, guidance, warmth and wisdom.
May God bless and keep you both.

Apple of His Eye

(Deuteronomy 32:10)

EVERYDAY USE: The "apple of his eye" is a phrase we call upon when we are trying to convey how important a certain person or object is to another person.

> He takes very good care of all his baseball cards, but his rookie card collection is really *the apple of his eye.*

> She has really changed his life. She brings out the best in him. I know that she is *the apple of his eye.*

You have probably heard many times that the apple is considered by many nutrition experts to be a "perfect food," having in it many of the nutrients needed to sustain healthy life. Not too unfamiliar is the phrase, "An apple a day keeps the doctor away."

The apple's perfection as a food is the likely reason it was chosen for this phrase. If you hold some things or some persons in such high regard that you feel they're practically perfect, they are the *apple of your eye.* Like so many of our modern everyday phrases, this phrase has its origin in the Bible.

BIBLE USE: One of the most amazing aspects of studying the biblical origin of our everyday phrases is the realization of just how old these phrases really are. Maybe you've only recently heard one of the phrases in this book. Yet the first time it was used was thousands of years ago.

That is the case with this phrase. Moses first employed it to convey to his people how dear they are to God.

> He found him in a desert land and in the wasteland, a howling wilderness; He encircled him, he instructed him, he kept him as the *apple of his eye.*

We see so many times in the Bible that the all-powerful God loves us so dearly! To be the apple of God's eye is the single greatest blessing we could hope to have!

ASK AND YOU SHALL RECEIVE

(Matthew 7::7)

EVERYDAY USE: How many times in everyday life, whether watching TV, or even in our own homes, do we hear this phrase? It usually comes in quick response to a request someone fulfills.

Mom, can I have another helping?

The mother replies,

Ask and you shall receive.

What could be easier? What a perfect world it would be if we quickly received anything we asked for! Or would it be perfect? What if people began to ask for things that only satisfied their own greed? In our human weakness would we always ask for the thing that would be best for us? We would if we truly understood the nature of this phrase as Jesus originally spoke it.

BIBLE USE: As believers our faith and our experience tell us that the one truly perfect thing that comes to us in our lives is the love of God. God's love comes to us from our families, our friends, and nature. One of the greatest truths that we can center on in our lives is that if we ask God to let us come closer, God will grant our prayer.

3

Ask, and you shall receive; seek, and you will find; knock, and the door will be opened to you.

Jesus goes on to say that if children asked their parents for something that would help them, the parents would quickly respond. How much more quickly, then, will God respond to the voice of his children who ask for divine love and help!

Be of Good Cheer

(John 16:33)

EVERYDAY USE: This particular phrase takes on many different forms in everyday use. Recently a talented singer named Bobby McFerrin shared a simple, sweet message with millions of people when he sang, "Don't worry, be happy," That's the central meaning of this familiar phrase from the Bible. In its original form the phrase was very popular with English speaking people from the sixteenth through the nineteenth centuries.

> With the holidays coming upon us, we should all *be of good cheer.*

> Take heart when times seem toughest; *be of good cheer.*

Isn't it amazing that sometimes even just hearing the words "be happy" or "cheer up" can begin to make us feel better? What nicer way to receive this encouragement than to receive it from our God!

BIBLE USE: Most of us have heard the Bible story of Jesus walking on water to meet his disciples in their boat on the sea. When the disciples saw the figure of Jesus walking on the water, they thought it was a' ghost. Jesus called out to them, saying:

> *Be of good cheer!* It is I; do not be afraid.

5

And again in John 16:33 Jesus prepares his disciples for the perils coming upon them.

> These things I have spoken to you, that in me
> you may have peace. In the world you will
> have tribulation; but *be of good cheer*, I have
> overcome the world.

In life we rarely know what awaits us around the next corner. Yet Jesus, who has perfect knowledge, tells us not to worry, to be of good cheer because God in heaven looks after us in all things. If we learn to trust in God, our lives will be filled with less worry and more happiness.

BEAR THE BURDEN

(Matthew 20:12)

EVERYDAY USE: Though we often hear the first part of this phrase, "bear the burden," in actuality the full phrase is, "bear the burden and the heat of the day." These words are an admonition to endure the stressful conditions and harsh physical demands of life.

> Others may take a holiday, while we must *bear the burden.*

> They are trying their best to work as a team, with every member contributing equal shares. Still, the team captain *bears the burden.*

Those who bear the burden usually take responsibility for their own actions, and the actions of others. The origin of this phrase comes from a parable in the Bible that in its brief span produced four of our most used modern phrases.

BIBLE USE: The parable of the workers in the vineyard offers a great deal of advice to us on how to conduct our lives. Upon reading through the parable we learn that God looks upon matters much differently than we do. The passage which contains the phrase we are examining shows the anger of the workers in the vineyard when a group of workers who started late in the day received the same pay as the workers who began their labors early in the day.

These last men have worked only one hour,
and you made them equal to us who have
borne the burden and the heat of the day.

Jesus taught many lessons about God's kingdom through parables. One of the messages this parable illustrates is that many people feel they are better than others because they have been following God's laws all their lives. Sometimes they feel they are somewhat better or more worthy than a person who has only recently come to believe and conduct their lives according to God's ways.

We must guard against such an attitude, remembering this parable. Instead of judging the faith of others, we should look for a chance to help one another *bear the burden*. Hardships in life can be made easier when we help one another to get through them.

THE BLIND LEADING
THE BLIND

(Matthew 15:14)

EVERYDAY USE: The image suggested by this phrase is that of one unsighted person trying to lead another unsighted person. However, the original use of this phrase was never intended to be demeaning to the visually impaired. Many unsighted people are extraordinarily capable of finding their way in the world today, as well as leading others.

> He's trying to teach her how to use the computer. Now that's the *blind leading the blind!*

> Neither of them knew how to get there, but they went anyway. You know what they say, the *blind leading the blind!*

The reference to being "blind" refers to a lack of knowledge or understanding, as in the phrase "blind to the dangers ahead." In many applications of this phrase the implication is that both parties lack knowledge. Therefore, how can one teach the other? Jesus' use of this phrase referred to the "spiritual blindness" suffered by some of the Pharisees in his day.

BIBLE USE: The circumstances surrounding this phrase from the Bible dealt with the Pharisees criticizing Jesus' disciples for not following the traditions of the elders. In particular, they were upset that Jesus'

disciples did not wash their hands when they ate bread!
Jesus pointed out to the Pharisees that it was they, the
Pharisees, who did not follow the traditions of the
elders. Jesus showed his listeners that many of the
things they were teaching were more form than content.
They went against the core teachings of God.

Later the disciples came to Jesus to tell him that
the Pharisees were offended by what Jesus had said. To
this, Jesus answered: "Every plant which my heavenly
Father has not planted will be uprooted" (Mt 15:13).
Then he added:

> Let them alone. They are *blind leaders of the
> blind*. And if the *blind leads the blind* both
> will fall into a ditch.

The blindness which Jesus refers to in this passage
is spiritual blindness. Remember how often Jesus refers
to the "light of God" and "seeing without seeing." The
"sight" Jesus so often refers to is *faith*. The light which
he so often speaks of is not physical light, but the divine
light of God. Some Pharisees did not have such vision.
That is why Jesus spoke of them as being "blind."

BOTTOMLESS PIT

(Revelation 9:1)

EVERYDAY USE: Even though we hear this phrase quite often, if one stops to think about it, it is hard to imagine a "bottomless pit"—a hole so deep and dark it seems to go on without end. In today's use, it is meant to exaggerate the depth of something.

> He eats so much, it's as if his stomach is a *bottomless pit*.

> She told our class that getting caught up in drugs is like being sucked into a bottomless pit.

In each of the examples we can see how this phrase is meant to convey something that seems to have no end. Let us see how the prophet John used this phrase in the book of Revelation.

BIBLE USE: The book of Revelation deals with the second coming of Jesus Christ. The prophet John writes down the visions that the angel of God caused him to see. In Revelation John describes his vision in this way:

> Then the fifth angel sounded his trumpet: And I saw a star fallen from heaven to the earth. To him was given the key to the *bottomless pit*.

The reference to the bottomless pit in the book of Revelation is to the notion that the troubles which will befall those not called to salvation will seem to have no end. They will long for relief, and will find none. The relief for believers is God's promise to call us all together in the life to come. God's goodness and mercy will endure forever.

Cast Your Bread Upon the Water

(Ecclesiastes 11:1)

EVERYDAY USE: It sounds like a soggy proposition if one takes that everyday phrase at face value. I remember hearing it most from my parents, especially my father. That's the true reason that these Bible phrases, along with their abiding truth and wisdom have kept their place in everyday use for thousands of years—people use them! Parents tell children, children grow to be parents, and then they tell their children!

Often I would ask my father his advice in a given situation. One of those conversations went something like this:

> Dad, I'd really like to go out for the basketball team this year, but if I don't make it, that would be really embarrassing.

And then my Dad answered:

> You'll never know if you are good enough to make the team until you try. You've worked very hard to get yourself ready for this. Now it's time to *cast your bread upon the water* and see what happens. Have some faith in yourself.

This particular phrase has several meanings and people us it in a variety of ways. To some it means:

"Take a chance and see what happens." To others it means: "Leave it to fate, do all you can do and let it go." In the Bible it takes on still one other meaning.

BIBLE USE: The book of Ecclesiastes contains a great many pearls of wisdom. If we let its ancient words speak to us, it will serve us very well in our daily lives. In this passage we are told:

> *Cast your bread upon the waters,* for you will find it after many days.

The advice given in Ecclesiastes is to share our wealth with others, without expecting to be repaid in any way. It is felt that if we lead a life of generosity and service to others, we will receive graces in our time of need.

Another way I was taught to think of this is that if every person in the world helped only one other person, then every person in the world would be helped.

Charity Begins at Home

(1 Timothy 5:8)

EVERYDAY USE: This is a fairly easy phrase to understand, and is often used in a joking manner.

> Now that you have all that money, remember, *charity begins at home.*

> It is all well and good to be helpful to strangers, but remember, *charity begins at home.*

If we really want to understand the right meaning of this phrase, we need only look at its biblical context.

BIBLE USE: A good thing to remember when reading St. Paul is that he was actually writing letters to those carrying on the work of the church in faraway places. He addressed the problems that the early missionaries were facing in their day-to-day lives. Some people were so anxious to be a part of the very important work of building the early Christian church that they felt it was acceptable to neglect their loved ones in favor of working for the church.

Here is St. Paul's response to this situation:

> But if anyone does not provide for his own, and especially for those of his household, he has denied the faith and is worse than an unbeliever.

17

We must realize that our witness to Christ must begin with the way we respect and treat the members of our own family. Charity should not mean simply the giving of money as modern culture has defined it. It must be expanded to mean that we must deal with one another in the spirit of giving. That is the true definition of *charity begins at home.*

CLIMBING THE WALLS

(Joel 2:7)

EVERYDAY USE: This phrase is often used to describe someone who is very restless and feeling caged up with nowhere to go and nothing to do. Feeling unable to change the course of certain events can also lead to the feeling that is expressed when we say, "Climbing the walls."

> He's been stuck inside so long, he's *climbing the walls.*

> Look at that poor mother. Her children have her *climbing the walls.*

As you can see, the usage of the phrase fits several different circumstances. The use in the Bible is more readily understood if one is aware of the context in which the phrase is used.

BIBLE USE: This passage is found in the book of Joel. In the preceding passages, Joel describes the land as being destroyed by locusts and drought because the inhabitants of the land spent their time in drinking and folly. Joel also depicts the great mourning people endured for the loss of all their earthly possessions.

In the verse which contains the original use of the phrase "climbing the walls," Joel is detailing the power of the army of the Lord. He tells of how they will sweep across the land.

They run like mighty men. They *climb the wall* like men of war. Everyone marches in formation, and they do not break ranks.

The Lord's army in this verse is able to climb walls or overcome any obstacle in their path, because they are focused on the will of God. When we become restless, and feel as though we're *climbing the walls,* perhaps it would help us if we try to center ourselves on the will of God in our lives.

CRY IN THE WILDERNESS

(Isaiah 40:3 & Matthew 3:3)

EVERYDAY USE: When someone is sending out a message that very few people are hearing, we say that the message is like "a cry in the wilderness." If you think about it, the phrase makes a lot of sense. If you were walking through a heavily wooded area calling out a message, not many people would hear you, would they? In modern terms the entanglement of cities and towns is sometimes referred to as a jungle or a wilderness. In a lot of cases, there are faithful messages being delivered in our cities and towns that are not being heard by very many people.

> In the late 1960s, the warnings about the dangers of cigarette smoking were like a *cry in the wilderness.*

> She reported to the class that the dangers of over-population are currently considered *a cry in the wilderness.*

Now let's look at the original meaning of this familiar phrase.

BIBLE USE: Isaiah speaks to the Israelites of a joyous time when the reign of God will replace the reign of unjust earthly kings. As he depicts this time of forgiveness from God, he encourages the Israelites to prepare their hearts for the coming of God's goodness.

The voice of one *crying in the wilderness,* "Prepare the way of the Lord; make straight in the desert a highway for our God."

In the New Testament, Matthew proclaims that John the Baptist is the one of whom Isaiah foretold:

For this is he who was spoken of by the prophet Isaiah saying, "The voice of one *crying in the wilderness,* "Prepare the way of the Lord; make his paths straight."

Sometimes in our lives, we feel that we are lost in a wilderness. Perhaps it is a wilderness of confusion, of pressures, or of conflicts. If we can learn to find a still moment in the course of our day, we may hear the voice of God crying from within our wilderness, assuring us of God's love and care. God's voice may even come through the voice of a friend or loved one, to lead us out of our own personal wildernesses.

Days Are Numbered

(Daniel 5:26)

EVERYDAY USE: If we think about it, we have probably all heard this phrase at one time or another in our daily lives. Maybe we've heard it in a cartoon where some villainous character is threatening someone:

> All right, I'm gonna get you. *Your days are numbered.*

Or maybe we've heard it on one of the popular police shows:

> We'll bring this criminal to justice. His *days are numbered.*

If we didn't know better, we might think of this as a modern phrase, the product of the imagination of the writers who create movie and cartoon scripts. In reality, this common phrase is over two thousand years old.

BIBLE USE: These words about one's days being numbered come from the book of Daniel. Daniel was a great prophet, and we know him as the one whose faith saved him from the lions' den. In fact, he's often referred to as "Daniel of the lions' den." In Daniel 5:26 we find the origin of this phrase.

> And this is what it means: God has *numbered the days* of your kingdom and brought it to an end.

We learn from many readings in the Bible that there is only a certain amount of time given to every purpose under heaven. We know from our day-to-day lives that school days are numbered, vacation days are numbered, the days of the seasons—winter, spring, summer, and fall—are all numbered. As believers we know that the time given us here on earth to do God's will is numbered too. For faithful people the phrase *your days are numbered* is one of good news. It means that when the numbered days run out, we will know everlasting peace and happiness.

Den of Thieves

(Jeremiah 7:11 and Matthew 21:12-13)

EVERYDAY USE: Here are a few examples of how we use this Bible phrase in our everyday lives:

> Tonight police broke into a high-rise building on the city's upper east side. What they discovered was that the building, though clean and serene-looking from the outside, was actually a *den of thieves.*

> She told the class that when they wander the streets alone at night, they are wandering through a *den of thieves.*

In whatever context we hear the phrase used, we certainly are left with the feeling that a den of thieves is no area in which we would want to find ourselves!

BIBLE USE: As you think about it, what could be further from a house of prayer than a den of thieves? We get an appreciation for Jesus' anger when he chases the money changers from God's temple in Matthew 21.

> Then Jesus went into the temple of God and drove out all those who bought and sold in the temple, and overturned the tables of the money changers and the seats of those who sold doves. And he said to them, "It is written, 'My house shall be called a house of prayer, but you have made it a *den of thieves.*'"

26

Imagine a handy bank machine in the back of your own church. Imagine merchants selling goods and haggling over prices while a church service is unfolding. We see all throughout the scriptures how sacred prayer was and is to sincere believers. When we enter our local house of worship we must try our best to have our thoughts center on God. We mustn't let anything or any thought steal time away from our prayers, our personal and communal dialogue with God.

DIVIDE THE SPOILS

(Isaiah 9:3)

EVERYDAY USE: You wouldn't think that something called "spoils" would have any value, would you? When I hear the word "spoils," I think people are referring to something that has gone bad, like meat, or cheese, or the last little bit of milk in the bottom of the carton that got pushed to the back of the refrigerator. I never once thought of "spoils" as anything having value. That's why I never quite understood the meaning of statements such as:

> To the victor go the *spoils*.

If I won something, I'd really be upset if the grand prize was a dinner of spoiled meat, cheese, and milk. Another phrase I have heard used in this way is:

> The *spoils* of war.

I always thought that last phrase was referring to the way everything was ruined during battle. As it turns out, one of the old meanings for the word "spoils" was "valuables, goods, or territory taken by war." The meaning is so old, in fact, that we find it in the Old Testament in the book of Isaiah.

BIBLE USE: In chapter 9 of Isaiah, the coming of a messiah is prophesied. Isaiah describes a government of peace that will have no end. In verse 3, he uses this phrase to describe the prosperity that will exist when God's kingdom is established.

You have multiplied a nation and increased its joy. They rejoice before you according to the joy of the harvest, as men rejoice when they *divide the spoil.*

Whenever I read or hear about things being "divided" or the "spoils of victory" I like to think of that time when we will all be united in perfect oneness, that time when no one will feel like a loser, nor that we must go without necessary things. Of course that time I am thinking of is the time we enter the kingdom of heaven, never to have anything *spoiled* again.

Drop in the Bucket

(Isaiah 40: 15)

EVERYDAY USE: Often we hear people use this phrase when they want to refer to a very small amount of something. If you think of it, a single drop is hardly noticeable in a big bucket of water. They might say something like:

> The price of this used bike is $10.00, but that's just a *drop in the bucket* compared to how much it's worth.

> We worked on this project all day, but it's just a *drop in the bucket* compared to what we have left to do.

BIBLE USE: In this passage the prophet Isaiah is telling the people how great God really is. He tells them that God will comfort them from all their earthly sorrows. One of the ways Isaiah chose to convey the greatness of God to the Israelites was to compare divine power and wisdom to earthly things. Close your eyes and picture all the nations of the world gathered together in one place, with all their armies, their weapons and their might. That would be an incredible gathering of power, wouldn't it?

Yet, as Isaiah tells the Israelites, all the nations' might and power are nothing compared to God's.

Behold, the nations are as a *drop in the bucket,* and are counted as the small dust on the scales.

The next time you hear someone use the phrase "a drop in the bucket," you'll know the real meaning of the phrase is that the power and greatness of humanity is but a drop in the bucket compared to the power, greatness and abiding love of God.

Eleventh Hour

(Matthew 20: 6)

EVERYDAY USE: Today people use the phrase "the eleventh hour" when they want to explain something that happened at the last possible moment. They'll say:

> The United States Congress passed a bill in *the eleventh hour* to avoid a confrontation over the federal deficit.

> The school board made an *eleventh hour* decision to keep schools open through the summer.

Have you ever wondered why the "eleventh hour has gotten so much attention and come to be such a significant time? We all know that there are twenty-four hours in a day, so why would the eleventh hour come to be so important? One answer comes from the Bible.

BIBLE USE: The eleventh hour has come to be significant because Jesus chose to use the eleventh hour in a parable about workers in a vineyard. If we study our everyday phrases, we will find that many of them either come directly from, or are directly related to, the wisdom of God spoken through the prophets.

In the parable Jesus tells of a landowner who goes out in the morning to hire laborers to work in his fields. He goes out again in the third hour, the ninth hour, and finally, as St. Matthew tells us:

And about the *eleventh hour* he went out and found others standing idle, and said to them, "Why have you been standing here idle all day?"

St. Matthew goes on to tell of how the landowner hires those laborers at the eleventh hour and sends them to work in his fields. When the work day is finished, he pays them the same as the first laborers he hired. They started late in the workday, and yet they received the full benefit of the day's wages. From this we have the everyday use of this phrase for things that happen at the last possible moment before a deadline.

While it is better if we do our work, including our work of faith, early and across the span of our lifetime, God is always ready to welcome, to love, and to forgive us—even at the *eleventh hour*.

EVIL EYE

(Matthew 20: 13-15)

EVERYDAY USE: If we didn't know better, we might think that the phrase "evil eye" is simply a part of Hollywood horror movies, an expression used to scare up images of ghosts and goblins. In other cases, the phrase is used to describe a look of intense disapproval or anger. In our day-to-day life we sometimes hear phrases such as:

> I think that she's very upset with him; she keeps giving him the *evil eye*.

> Boy, that person just gave me the *evil eye*, and I don't know why.

BIBLE USE: If we examine the biblical origin of this phrase, we can find that it carries an important lesson for us all. The passage in which this phrase appears is a parable about the workers in the vineyard. The phrase is used near the end of the parable when the laborers who had been hired early in the morning were complaining that the laborers who had come close to the end of the day were being paid the same wages. To understand its context we should listen to the verses just before it.

> But he answered one of them and said, "Friend, I am doing you no wrong. Did you not agree with me for a denarius? Take what is yours and go your way. I wish to give to this

35

last man the same as you. Is it not lawful for me to do what I wish with my own things? Or is your *evil eye* because I am good?

Sometimes we may think we have every right to be angry with various people. We may feel they have done something against us and so we shoot an angry, disapproving look in their direction. In reality, such persons may not have meant to harm us or cause us ill feelings in any way. They may simply have been doing what they felt was right. Or, in some instances, our "evil eye" says more about our own jealousy than about any evil done by another.

The next time we're tempted to give someone the *evil eye* we should pause. Often kind words or a candid exchange of ideas will resolve differences far better than grudges or evil looks.

FALL BY THE WAYSIDE

(Matthew 13:3-4)

EVERYDAY USE: All of us have many hopes, dreams, and plans for our lives. Some of these dreams and plans we pursue with every ounce of our strength and dedication, and some we decide aren't as important as we thought they were. We say that those we feel are no longer important *fell by the wayside.*

> We had made plans to change the old building into a recreation center, but the plans *fell by the wayside.*

> Many people felt that he had tremendous potential, but he seems to have let his talent *fall by the wayside.*

The phrase relates to the failure to reach a goal that was well within one's grasp. It comes from a parable about potential and goals with which we are all familiar.

BIBLE USE: Isn't it amazing that the prophets and Jesus spoke to simple farmers, servants, and townspeople thousands of years ago, and yet their teachings still have such impact on the lives of modern people? Of course this is so because God's wisdom is eternal and perfect.

There is wisdom in the scripture that is as timely and nourishing today as when it was first written. Jesus chose this image of a sower sowing seeds because the spark of spirituality alive in us all is like a seed that must bear fruit if we are to enjoy eternal happiness.

Then He spoke many things to them in parables, saying: "Behold, a sower went out to sow. And as he sowed, some seed *fell by the wayside;* and the birds came and devoured them."

We needn't feel that our seed from God is falling by the wayside. God is ever before us to help us grow. All God asks of us is to sow love, to try our best, and to strive to grow. And the parable promises a harvest of thirty-, sixty-, or even a hundred-fold.

FALL FROM GRACE

(Galatians 5:4)

EVERYDAY USE: In our modern world we often hear newscasters proclaim that a certain public figure or celebrity has experienced a "fall from grace" because of some personal failing or other. We may hear news releases like:

> The aging movie queen, winner of numerous film awards, has recently had a *fall from grace* when it was revealed that she often acts as a tyrant.

> The Senator was riding a tide of popularity until a recent investigation uncovered his misconduct. Now his *fall from grace* is happening as quickly as his rise to fame.

"Grace" in many modern applications refers to the position of popularity one holds within a certain community. Grace is equal in meaning to "favor" or "approval." While these meanings do have application in a modern sense, the original meaning of "grace" is what St. Paul is referring to in his letter to the Galatians.

BIBLE USE: As I grew up, I remember hearing that "the will of God will never take you where the grace of God can't reach you." God's grace is that all-powerful factor or spark of divine life which can bring us successfully through any earthly trial or hardship. God's "grace" is a "favor." Imagine then what a tragedy it would be to fall from true grace, a condition St. Paul describes.

> You have become estranged from Christ, you
> who attempt to be justified by the law; you
> have *fallen from grace.*

As we go through our daily lives, we should be confident that like children we can call upon the "grace of God" to see us through the hardships in our lives. As long as we look to God for all things, even though we may have our failings, we will not fall from his grace. It is the grace of God which we should be concerned about, not the grace or fame of this world.

FEET OF CLAY

(Daniel 2:32-34)

EVERYDAY USE: I always understood "feet phrases" fairly easily—phrases like "cold feet," "hot feet," "dancing feet," "happy feet," and "feet first." The one I always stubbed my toe on was "feet of clay." For all the world, I couldn't understand the reference of "feet of clay" in statements like:

> He was head of the military and ran his country like a dictator, but like most tyrants, he had *feet of clay*.

> They felt that they could go on winning championships forever. Yet today, in the face of an unknown opponent, they showed that they had *feet of clay*.

What of this reference to playdough peds? Where did it come from, and what did or does it signify? The answer can be found in the book of Daniel.

BIBLE USE: The answer always seems obvious once someone tells it to you. When I learned the reason behind this reference I gave a customary nod of my head, accompanied by that familiar phrase, "Oh yeah, of course, I should have known."

If you wanted to forge an invincible sword, you would most likely forge it from steel or iron. If you made it from clay, I am sure you can imagine the difference. If it is said of someone that he or she has "feet of clay" it

41

means that this person has a weakness, a vulnerability. The reference is taken from the second chapter of Daniel wherein he explains to King Nebuchadnezzar the nature of his dream.

This image's head was of fine gold, its chest and arms of silver, its belly and thighs of bronze, its legs of iron, its *feet partly of iron and partly of clay*. You watched while a stone was cut out without hands, which struck the image on its feet of iron and clay, and broke them in pieces.

Daniel was telling the king that while his kingdom was strong, those that followed his would be weak, for they would not be based on righteousness or righteous living. We must be careful that we attach our loyalty and love not to things that will be fleeting and crumble under stress, but to those that will endure in good times and in bad.

First Shall Be Last and Last Shall Be First

(Matthew 20:16)

EVERYDAY USE: I don't know if you've ever done this, but when I was growing up and found myself on the short side of a situation, like being the last picked, or the last one left so I was "it" for a game of tag, I always invoked this great saying, "First shall be last and last shall be first—I call!"

"I call." The first one who shouted that got to make the rules in our neighborhood. We'd say the silliest things, then add the magical "I call," so that whatever we said became law.

> No tagging people with your left hand on the right side of their body if you're standing on the north side of the street because the shadows are longer there—I call! Oh, and *first shall be last and last shall be first,* I call.

When I was growing up, I never knew that the phrase I used to get myself out of last place was actually a biblical phrase.

BIBLE USE: The Bible offers us a glimpse of the great difference between the way we see things and the way God sees them. God sees things in their true nature.

In the parable of the vineyard workers, Jesus tells how angry a group of workers were because they worked all day long and received the same wages as men who worked only an hour. In the eyes of the first group of laborers, this was totally unfair. In the eyes of the landowner, it was perfectly fair.

To understand the true nature of this familiar phrase, we must listen to the entire verse which contains the phrase.

> *So the last shall be first, and the first last.* For many are called, but few chosen.

We must guard against thinking that we are better than other people because we go to church and they don't. We must resist feeling full of self-importance because we know so much about God and other people may not. Knowledge of God is one thing, closeness to God is often another. Scripture teaches us that a humble heart will keep us close to God. As Jesus once suggested, it is better to sit at the foot of the table and be invited to the front, than to sit at the front and be asked to leave.

Flesh and Blood

(Matthew 16:14-17)

EVERYDAY USE: The meaning of this phrase is relatively clear. When we invoke the term "flesh and blood" we are referring to someone who is related. The term can also be used to indicate a living person.

> Many think that she is so mean she would throw her own *flesh and blood* out into the cold.

> I'm a human being, just as you are. I am *flesh and blood* like you. All I ask is that you show me the same respect I show you.

The term is not a particularly difficult one to understand. TV shows, movies, paperback novels, and pop songs all make use of the phrase. We hear it numerous times during the course of everyday life. Yet, how many of us are familiar with the way in which Jesus used this phrase?

BIBLE USE: As you might imagine, Jesus caused quite a stir in his public life. Debates raged among the people of Israel as to whether or not Jesus was the messiah. The leaders argued among themselves; fathers argued with sons and mothers debated with daughters. On one particular occasion Jesus asked his disciples who the people were saying he was.

45

So they said, "Some say John the Baptist, some Elijah, and others Jeremiah or one of the prophets." He said to them. "But who do you say that I am?" Simon Peter answered and said, "You are the Christ, the Son of the living God." Jesus answered and said to him, "Blessed are you, Simon Bar-Jonah, for *flesh and blood* has not revealed this to you, but my Father who is in heaven.

It is our flesh and blood that makes us human. Throughout his life on earth Jesus sought to teach the people that while we are made of flesh and blood our true nature is one of spirit. It is our spirit that makes us children of God. We must honor and care for our *flesh and blood,* for it was chosen by God to be the earthly home of our divine spirit.

Four Corners
of the Earth

(Revelation 7:1)

EVERYDAY USE: If people say today that they are willing to travel to the "four corners of the earth" for something, they are saying that they will travel into the most remote regions of our world. Obviously, since the world is round it does not have four corners.

> I would travel to the *four corners of the earth* if I could have her for my bride.

> You'll have to travel to the *four corners of the earth* to find a better friend than John.

When the thought was originally expressed, people of the day still believed that the world was flat. Therefore, *the four corners of the earth* would have been the most remote regions. That is why the author of the gospel of John chose the expression nearly two thousand years ago.

BIBLE USE: The book of Revelation (much as the name suggests) reveals the visions that John had concerning the end of the world. The book is full of images of the sweeping power of God almighty descending over the face of the earth. In this passage, John speaks of the angels of God coming to protect God's children. He begins the passage with this familiar phrase:

Four Corners of The Earth

After these things I saw four angels standing at the *four corners of the earth,* holding the four winds of the earth, that the wind should not blow on the earth, on the sea, or on any tree.

Another of the images John speaks of deals with the world's condition **after** the evil has been banished from the earth. John writes in Revelation 21:1: "Then I saw a new heaven and a new earth, for the first heaven and the first earth had passed away." Then in Revelation 21:4 he gives us the most magnificent news: "And God will wipe away every tear from their eyes; there shall be no more death, nor sorrow, nor crying. There shall be no more pain, for the former things have passed away." What great news John *reveals* to us. We can have the happiness described in his words if we have God at the center of our lives every day, and then we will share in that eternal kingdom that encompasses the *four corners of the earth.*

Good Samaritan

(Luke 10:31-34)

EVERYDAY USE: When you think about it, it's actually rather ironic that this phrase, which comes from a story about traveling, is most often invoked in everyday use while people are "on the road." You might hear things said like:

> Oh great! This is just great! We're stuck in rush hour traffic, and this guy is letting everyone ahead of him. Just my luck—stuck behind a *good Samaritan*.

Who was the original good Samaritan? Do you recall what he did to earn such fame that he is still remembered and his image is invoked centuries after he lived?

BIBLE USE: The parable of the good Samaritan is one of the more widely known parables from the Bible. It is certainly one worth reflecting upon. The parable of the good Samaritan tells of a man who was traveling from Jerusalem to Jericho when he fell in among thieves who stripped him, beat him, and left him for dead. In verses 31 and 32 we read of certain self-righteous men who walked right passed the wounded man.

> Now by chance a certain priest came down that road. And when he saw him, he passed by on the other side. Likewise a Levite, when he arrived at that place, came and looked, and

passed by on the other side. But a certain Samaritan, as he journeyed, came where he was. And when he saw him, he had compassion. So he went to him and bandaged his wounds, pouring on oil and wine; and he set him on his own animal, brought him to an inn, and took care of him.

One of the lessons I have learned from this parable is that sometimes one has to look for ways to be of service to others. There will be times when helping others will come painlessly and pleasantly, such as when we lend a quick helping hand, assist someone we like, or share an easy smile with a weary friend. Other times it will require personal sacrifice and perhaps a certain degree of discomfort or inconvenience. When I hear the phrase *"good Samaritan"* used, I always say a quick prayer that God will give me the courage to help others when they need me, even if it means a little inconvenience for me.

Handwriting on the Wall

(Daniel 5:5)

EVERYDAY USE: When people speak about seeing the "handwriting on the wall", they are saying that it is obvious to them that a certain event is bound to take place. Usually the phrase is associated with something serious.

> When the team lost fifteen games in a row, the *handwriting on the wall* spelled out doom for the coach.

> The *handwriting on the wall* tells me that unless we move quickly, something terrible is bound to happen.

Let's take a moment to learn how this phrase came into existence.

BIBLE USE: This phrase comes to us from the book of Daniel. In this story, King Belshazzar threw a feast for a thousand of his lords. They were drinking wine to excess, and what is worse, they were drinking it out of vessels which were from the holy temple in Jerusalem. In the middle of this feast, we are told that a hand appeared and wrote some words into the plaster.

The king became very troubled by this incident. He summoned all of his magicians and astrologers, but none could decipher the meaning of the words. That is when he called upon Daniel to interpret the words. He offered Daniel a purple robe and a gold chain if he could interpret the words for him.

> In the same hour the fingers of a man's hand appeared and wrote opposite the lampstand on the plaster of the wall of the king's palace; and the king saw the part of the hand that wrote.

The end result of this action described was obviously the *handwriting on the wall*. When Daniel interpreted the handwriting for the king he informed him that the words spelled doom for the king and his kingdom. That is why when people refer to the handwriting on the wall they are referring to a sign of doom, "telling it like it is," even though the news is bad. It is an omen, one last warning, of what is likely to come.

HOUSE DIVIDED AGAINST ITSELF CANNOT STAND

(Matthew 12:25)

EVERYDAY USE: If by chance I was chosen to be on a game show of some kind, with the opportunity to win fabulous prizes, I would have lost if all I had to do was answer the following little question:

> Who said, *"A house divided against itself cannot stand"*?

I would have lost because I would have answered immediately that the author of the phrase "a house divided against itself cannot stand" was Abraham Lincoln. It wasn't. Jesus was the first to use the phrase. President Lincoln made reference to it in one of his famous speeches.

I shouldn't be surprised that President Lincoln would make reference to Jesus' words. He was president through one of the darkest and most difficult periods of this nation's history, and he leaned on his faith daily. When he used Jesus' words he was trying to heal the wounds that our nation endured when one section of our country fought against another section. But how did Jesus use and intend these words?

BIBLE USE: Even as Jesus spoke, he knew that his words would live on to give direction to his followers. Many of the situations that existed in Jesus' day still exist today. In this passage Jesus is answering the criticism of those who did not believe that he was the Son of God. They accused him of being the devil and, at the same time, of being able to cast out devils.

> But Jesus knew their thoughts, and said to them, "Every kingdom divided against itself is brought to desolation, and every city or *house divided against itself will not stand.*"

Jesus goes on to say to the people that those who are not with him are against him. Many times in life we are called upon to make decisions or answer criticisms about our behavior. Sometimes it causes a division within ourselves as to what would be the best course to take. We shouldn't allow ourselves to be anxious in such times of indecision. We should try to calm our thoughts by focusing on God in our lives. When we can do this, we find that the feeling of unity often overwhelms the feeling of division. It is when we feel unified in ourselves and our purpose in life that we make the best choices.

In the Twinkling of an Eye

(1 Corinthians 15:52)

EVERYDAY USE: When something happens so quickly that one can hardly believe one's eyes, people say it happened *"in the twinkling of an eye."* After all, the thinking goes, it couldn't have happened while one was watching, so it must have happened when one blinked.

Take a moment and look around your room. You probably know where everything in your room is (or maybe you don't). Now blink your eyes. The room looks the same, doesn't it? What would you think if, when you opened your eyes after just one blink, your room was totally different? It would be amazing, wouldn't it? It would hardly be believable. When you told people about it, you would probably say, "It happened *in the twinkling of an eye.*"

Sometimes people will say things like:

I saw him standing right there, and then he was gone, *in the twinkling of an eye.*

Everything was going along fine, but it all changed, *in the twinkling of an eye.*

BIBLE USE: St. Paul chose to use this phrase to explain to the Corinthians and, by extension, to all believers, that the final victory will be swift and complete. Many early Christians wanted to know when the Lord would return in glory. St. Paul answered by saying:

> In a moment, *in the twinkling of an eye*, at the last trumpet. For the trumpet will sound, and the dead will be raised incorruptible, and we shall be changed.

When we are waiting for a special day to arrive, whether it be a holiday, our birthday, or summer vacation, we sometimes begin to wonder if the event will ever happen. We really needn't wonder how soon we will be joined with all of our loved ones, in the company of God. It will happen quickly. It will seem as if it happened *in the twinkling of an eye.*

LABOR OF LOVE

(1 Thessalonians 1:2)

EVERYDAY USE: We hear this phrase used in our daily lives as an explanation for why someone might work so hard on a particular project or for a particular reason.

> She works hard all day long for her family. But she told me she doesn't mind because she considers it a *labor of love*.

> I don't know why anyone would work so hard for so little money. It must be a *labor of love*.

A "labor of love" is something we say when we are indicating that a person's motive for taking on a big task is not money, but love. Often people will take on a task that seems to be too much for others because they *love* the work.

Here again we see love's power. Even at a time when materialism is at its height of appeal and influence, the greatest things that we achieve are still accomplished through *labors of love*. Raising and caring for our families, finding cures for illness, reaching solutions for world conflict, and caring for one another— these are the greatest human accomplishments.

BIBLE USE: The work of spreading the early gospel was hard work indeed. The early disciples met resistance at every step. Controversy and arguments were their constant companions. They were chased out of many towns and threatened with death in others. Still, they loved the work of spreading the word of God. In his first letter to the Thessalonians, St. Paul applauds their efforts.

> We give thanks to God always for you all, making mention of you in our prayers, remembering without ceasing your work of faith, *labor of love,* and patience of hope in our Lord Jesus Christ in the sight of our God and Father.

When we are faced with a task that seems too big or too much trouble, we must try to center our thoughts on something we love. We could think of our families, our friends, and especially our God. If we fill our thoughts with feelings of love, the most troublesome tasks will go by without our even noticing them.

LAND OF MILK AND HONEY

(Exodus 3:8)

EVERYDAY USE: It has been many centuries since items such as milk and honey represented all the good one's heart could desire. If we reflect on these words we realize how little ancient peoples had to make their lives comfortable. To such people it was considered a great privilege to have good and basic things in life like milk and honey. In today's usage, the phrase depicts a situation rich with opportunity and good fortune.

> He's simply looking for the easy way out. He wants to spend his days in *the land of milk and honey.*

> When I retire I'd like to live in a farmhouse on about ten acres of land. To me that would be *the land of milk and honey.*

BIBLE USE: This is one of the more famous quotes often borrowed from the Bible. It comes from the book of Exodus, which marks the days of Moses and the calling of the Israelites by God to live according to the commandments. In this passage, Moses hears the voice of God speaking to him from the burning bush. God tells Moses of the divine plans for the chosen people, and in doing so God says:

> So I have come down to deliver them out of the hand of the Egyptians, and to bring them up from that land to a good and large land, to *a*

land flowing with milk and honey, to the place of the Canaanites and the Hittites and the Amorites and the Perizzites and the Hivites and the Jebusites.

The phrase *a land flowing with milk and honey* was chosen by God to represent all the goodness that the hearts of the Israelites could desire. We should ask ourselves: What phrase might God choose to speak to us today? What phrase would represent all goodness in our world? As we answer that question, it may help us to decide if our priorities are in the right order.

Last Gasp

(2 Maccabees 7:9)

EVERYDAY USE: This is such a popular phrase that it may surprise you to learn that it has biblical origins. We hear it used quite often in the broadcasting of sporting events, or on the nightly news.

> The rescue workers made a *last gasp* attempt to find the child in the burning building. Cheers arose from the onlookers when the fire fighters emerged from the building with the little girl in their arms.

> The home team has rallied after being down fifteen points. It's going to take a heroic *last gasp* effort for them to pull out a victory in this one.

The phrase's use in the Bible depicts a true life and death situation.

BIBLE USE: The Hebrew scriptures relate many stories of how the Israelites were persecuted for their belief in God. One story taken from 2 Maccabees tells of seven brothers who were put to death for their refusal to partake of pork, a meat forbidden by their custom. In the Bible's account, each brother is brutally tortured for his refusal to eat the pork. Here are the words of the second brother to the king who was persecuting his family.

With his *last gasp* he exclaimed, "Cruel brute, you may discharge us from this present life, but the king of the world will raise us up, since we die for his laws, to live again forever.

Whatever small hardships we endure in this life, whether they be physical hardships, misunderstanding from friends, or the awkward feeling of taking an unpopular stand, we must realize that fidelity to the end, even with our last breath, is essential for a sense of integrity here, and for eternal peace hereafter.

LEFT HAND DOESN'T KNOW WHAT THE RIGHT HAND IS DOING

(Matthew 6:3-4)

EVERYDAY USE: This phrase is commonly used to illustrate a state of confusion that exists within a group of people when one portion of the group does something completely opposite of another portion of the same group.

> That team is playing very poorly right now. It's as though *the left hand doesn't know what the right hand is doing.*

> I know why that company is struggling to stay in business. It is because *the left hand doesn't know what the right hand is doing.*

Try a little experiment for a moment. Try tying both of your shoelaces at the same time. Or try the playground game of rubbing your stomach with one hand while tapping the top of your head with the other hand. If you've ever tried either of these activities you'll get a quick idea of the confusion that exists when the left hand tries to do the opposite of the right hand. As true as this application of the phrase is, it is not exactly what was originally meant. To understand the true meaning of this phrase we must turn to Matthew 6:3-4.

BIBLE USE: In this passage Jesus is teaching his disciples and followers the proper spirit with which we should do good deeds. Jesus tells us that when we do a good deed it should be done and offered in love to God in heaven. He tells us to guard against doing good deeds just so other people will see that you've done them and say nice things about you.

> But when you do a charitable deed, do not let your *left hand know what your right hand is doing,* that your charitable deed may be in secret; and your Father who sees in secret will himself reward you openly.

We see then that Jesus told us a different meaning from the one we commonly use. In everyday life this phrase from the Bible means a state of confusion. However, Jesus used it to tell us to keep our charitable acts a secret. Your good deeds will mean more to you and to God if they are done in loving silence.

Little Bird Told Me

LITTLE BIRD TOLD ME

(Ecclesiastes 10:20)

EVERYDAY USE: When people have discovered something but don't want anyone else to know where they got their information, they will often say, "a little bird told me." For example, we often hear phrases like these:

> A *little bird told me* it's your birthday today.

> You may be wondering how I found out where you've been. Well, *a little bird told me.*

As you can imagine, there are countless little birds filling the air around us. By using this phrase, we are saying we got our information from a secret source that we are not going to reveal.

BIBLE USE: This phrase is an example of how a thought or concept originally expressed in the Bible has found its way into our everyday lives. Though the wording of the phrase has been altered somewhat, the thought is first recorded in the book of Ecclesiastes.

> Do not curse the king, even in your thought;
> do not curse the rich, even in your bedroom;
> for *a bird of the air* may carry your voice, and
> a bird in flight may tell the matter.

The message of this passage is a powerful one for us, even though we live thousands of years after it was originally spoken. What the passage is saying is that we should choose our words wisely because we never know who may be listening. Our words are often carried forth to others, as though by "little birds," and the person whom we are speaking about may come to know what we've said. Therefore, we should speak with wisdom, kindness, and honesty.

Makes Your Hair Stand on End

(Job 4:13-15)

EVERYDAY USE: Modern movie makers have been very successful at producing films that cause the sensation of *making your hair stand on end*. It is a feeling that occurs when one is very startled or frightened. What happens is that goose pimples come over us and raise the hairs around them. Literally our hair stands on end.

> That movie was so scary it *made my hair stand on end*.

> Wait until you get to the next chapter. It *makes your hair stand on end*.

But is this sensation brand new? Not really. The book of Job described this sensation thousands of years ago.

BIBLE USE: It is not Job but Eliphaz the Temanite who actually speaks the phrase with which we have become so familiar. He is describing to Job a vision of God's wrath.

> In disquieting thoughts from the visions of the night when deep sleep falls on men, fear came upon me, and trembling, which made all my

bones shake. Then a spirit passed before my face; *the hair on my body stood up.*

It is often surprising to learn that the words which we choose to express ourselves in modern life are often the same words used thousands of years ago. What is important to realize is that the original fear expressed by Eliphaz was fear of the wrath of God against the unjust. When one considers the frightening wrath of righteousness it is truly enough to *make your hair stand on end.*

MAN AFTER MY OWN HEART

(1 Samuel 13:13-14)

EVERYDAY USE: While growing up I heard my father use this phrase all of the time. Now I hear myself using it too. In reality that is exactly how a great deal of our idioms and maxims are handed down—by word of mouth. It is amazing to realize just how old some of our everyday phrases are. One has to consider that the reason these phrases have survived for so long (many in their original context) is that the truth they represent remains a truth for all time. I used to hear my father say things like:

> He enjoys a quiet evening after a hard day's work. He's a *man after my own heart*.

> You've brought me chocolate covered cherries and cold milk. You're *a man after my own heart*.

If you were to say to someone, "You're a man after my own heart," you'd be telling that person that he or she shares similar outlooks and opinions with you. This particular phrase from the Bible has kept much of its original meaning.

BIBLE USE: This phrase comes to us from the book of Samuel. The people of Israel had gone to Samuel when he was old and told him that they wanted a new king.

Samuel prayed to the Lord to heed the voice of the people. It was then that God chose Saul to lead the people. When Saul offered an unlawful sacrifice, Samuel came to him with these words.

> And Samuel said to Saul, "You have done foolishly. You have not kept the commandment of the Lord your God, which he commanded you. For now the Lord would have established your kingdom over Israel forever. But now your kingdom shall not continue. The Lord has sought for himself *a man after his own heart,* and the Lord has commanded him to be commander over his people, because you have not kept what the Lord commanded you.

When we keep the commandments of the Lord we are following the wishes of God's heart. As believers we learn to honor God's will because we know it is best for us. We all strive to be people *after his own heart.*

Man of Few Words

(Ecclesiastes 5:1-2)

EVERYDAY USE: I wish this were true of me. Unfortunately, I have always been one who used many words, not few. Just ask my grade school teachers. When I think of the people that I most admire in the world, they were those people who let their actions speak for their beliefs. Even Hollywood portrays its action heroes as men and women who prefer action to words.

> You won't hear her say much. Being a *woman of few words,* she prefers to let her actions speak for her beliefs.

> He is truly a *man of few words.* When he does speak, he commands attention.

Once again the tried and true wisdom of the Bible prophets holds fast through countless generations.

BIBLE USE: The author of Ecclesiastes is giving advice to the people of his day on how to conduct oneself in an upright way.

> Walk prudently when you go to the house of God; and draw near to hear rather than to give the sacrifice of fools, for they do not know that they do evil. Do not be rash with your mouth, and let not your heart utter anything

hastily before God. For God is in heaven, and you on earth; therefore, *let your words be few.*

If we think of those people we know who let themselves get carried away in idle chatter, spreading rumors and false witness, we know they are not people of few words. Certainly we do not have to count our words each day, but we should choose them carefully.

Mark My Words

(Isaiah 28:23)

EVERYDAY USE: This phrase is often invoked as a way of making a prediction. One of the meanings of the word "mark" is "to take notice, to heed"; so, then, to "mark my words" is to take heed of them

> You *mark my words*, mister, this fight isn't over yet.

> I have a feeling this group of young people can accomplish great things; you can *mark my words* on that.

The phrase can be associated with pleasant predictions or unpleasant ones. Mostly, in our daily use, it is invoked when people want to receive credit for a particular opinion they feel they were the first to voice. Let us hear how the prophet Isaiah used the phrase.

BIBLE USE: Isaiah often enjoined the people of Israel to heed the words of the Lord. He kept a constant vigil over the people's behavior so that he could direct them to avoid wrongdoing. In this particular passage he was speaking to the people, imploring them to listen to the teaching of God.

> Give ear and hear my voice, *listen and hear my speech.*

"Hear my speech" is largely considered the origin of the phrase *mark my words*. The words differ depending upon how one translates the original Hebrew. However, the meaning remains the same. Isaiah goes on to tell the people that listening to the teachings of God about the matters of our souls is no different than listening to instructions for plowing a field. If one does not properly plow and sow a field, how can one expect a crop to flourish? In the same way, Isaiah proclaims, if we do not heed the words of our God, telling us how we should live daily, how can we expect to share in the harvest of eternal life?

To "mark the words" of the prophets, who speak on God's behalf, is to heed them. The more we heed and live by those words, the more abundant and fruitful our lives will be.

NO REST FOR THE WICKED

(Isaiah 48:22)

EVERYDAY USE: This phrase is most often heard in daily use as a comment one makes about oneself.

> After I finish redoing the driveway, I have to rake the yard, trim the trees, clean the gutters, and paint the shutters. *No rest for the wicked,* I guess.

> The boss just told me I can't leave tonight until the report is finished. If that isn't bad enough, I have to come in on Saturday and do another report. You know what they say—*no rest for the wicked.*

The comment in today's vernacular is one that is meant to say, "I must be evil and that is why I am burdened with so much work." Actually, the original intent was somewhat different than the present day use.

BIBLE USE: The promise awaiting all faithful people at the end of their time on earth is the promise of eternal peace and rest in God. That is the rest referred to in this phrase. It is not rest, as in a break from labor or activity, but rest as in eternal peace. Isaiah reminds the Israelites not to lose sight of our ultimate goal in life by falling into idolatrous living.

> *"There is no peace,"* says the Lord, *"for the wicked."*

Most people who use this phrase in the modern sense are not saying that they feel they will have no place in the eternal kingdom with God. They are simply saying that they feel overworked and are unable to get enough time for adequate rest.

When we hear this phrase in our daily lives, maybe we can let it serve to remind us, in a more positive manner, that a glorious state of happiness awaits us at the end of our labors here on earth.

Nothing New Under the Sun

(Ecclesiastes 1:9)

EVERYDAY USE: When I began researching the origins of the common everyday phrases we use, I really came to believe that there is nothing new under the sun. I had the idea that much of modern language usage was just that—modern. But I have received an education quite to the contrary. I thought my parents were the originators of most of these phrases.

The more things change, the more they stay the same. There's really *nothing new under the sun.*

She thinks that she has some great secret, but believe me, with her there is *nothing new under the sun.*

If you think about it, the sun has seen about everything that has ever transpired on the earth. Humanity is constantly coming up with inventions that are in fact brand new, but the fact that humans are inventive is *nothing new under the sun.* Even the phrase itself is thousands of years old.

BIBLE USE: The book of Ecclesiastes is one of the most beautiful in the Bible. The simple, all-embracing wisdom offered in its passages have inspired many generations. In the 1960s a rock band called The Birds recorded a popular song whose lyrics came word-for-word from the book of Ecclesiastes. It was a song called "Turn Turn Turn" and its lyrics come from Ecclesiastes, chapter 3, verses 1-8. The phrase we are speaking of now comes from Ecclesiastes 1:9:

That which has been is what will be,
that which is done is what will be done
and there is *nothing new under the sun.*

The words of Ecclesiastes were written by "The Preacher." In this book of the Bible, the Preacher is saying that people in general are vain. Most act as if they believe that they are the first wise people on earth. He notices that every generation which comes along tries to forget the generation that preceded it. He wishes that people would listen more to the wisdom of the ages.

Perhaps this is the way our parents feel at times when they are trying to give us advice based on their experience. For as much as we may feel our lives are different from that of our parents, maybe we should reflect for a moment that there is *nothing new under the sun,* and that perhaps there is real value in listening to the wisdom gained by those who have walked life's roads before us.

ON ROCKY GROUND

(Matthew 13:5-6)

EVERYDAY USE: One hears many varieties of this expression in daily life

> We were moving along just fine until we hit some *rocky ground.*

> You really gave him some very sound advice, But I am afraid it fell on *rocky ground.*

In each case the phrase is depicting a situation that is less than desirable. When one thinks of "smooth sailing: or "fertile ground," one is imagining the best conditions for growth. When one thinks of obstacles and hindrances, the picture of rocky, uneven ground comes to mind.

BIBLE USE: The central beauty of all the parables that Jesus told was his ability to relate concepts of spirituality in ways that the common people could understand. Before Jesus walked among us, the matters of scripture and God's law belonged only to the more learned (at least that is how the learned perceived it.)

Jesus came to open the way to God for all of us. Because so many people of his day were farmers, they understood the concept of sowing seeds. Jesus then related the word of God as a seed sown by a sower. The phrase "rocky ground" comes from the parable of the sower wherein Jesus says:

Some fell *on stony places* where they did not have much earth; and they immediately sprang up because they had no depth of earth. But when the sun was up they were scorched, and because they had no root they withered away.

The parable teaches us to be receptive to the word of God and to nourish ourselves with prayer and moral living so that the seed of God's love within us will prosper and grow. The parable also explains how we should be wary of passing fancies, things that spring up quickly but do not last, like the seed that fell on rocky ground. It sprang up quickly, and withered just as quickly. Many things in our life come along at a moment's notice, only to fade away in the next moment. We will do best to devote ourselves to things that last, like our families, our homes, and our faith.

OUT OF THE MOUTHS OF BABES

(Psalm 8:1-2)

EVERYDAY USE: Small children are an endless source of amazement to adults when they utter phrases that are totally unexpected. If you have any younger brothers or sisters, maybe they have stunned your family at one time or another by saying something no one knew they knew! It often allows for moments of humor.

When the teacher asked Carl to recite the pledge of allegiance Carl perked right up and began: "I pledge allegiance to the flag of the United States of America. And to the republic for Rich's dad." It was so funny. You know what they say—*out of the mouths of babes.*

The phrase is a way of expressing the idea that children say the most unexpected things. The psalmist had a little different use in mind when he first used this phrase in the Bible.

BIBLE USE: In Psalm 8 the glory of the Lord in creation is being detailed. The psalm recounts how all of nature gives glory to God in its splendid visage. The psalmist is proclaiming that all of creation knows how excellent the Lord is. Even a nursing infant not yet old enough to stand on his own knows the excellence of God.

O Lord our Lord, how excellent is your name in all the earth; you have set your glory above the heavens!

Out of the mouths of babes and nursing infants you have ordained strength because of your enemies, that you may silence the enemy and the avenger.

Children do give glory to God in their innocent beauty. The psalmist is using a theme that Jesus used often in his teachings; that we must be childlike in our love of God. If you think about it, children are very expressive with their feelings. Feelings of joy or sorrow flow freely from them. When we feel happy about all that God has done for us in our lives, we should let those feelings flow from us as they do *out of the mouths of babes.*

POWERS THAT BE

(Romans 13:1)

EVERYDAY USE: The first time I became acquainted with this phrase I was reading a book on world governments entitled, *The Powers That Be*. I thought the author of the book was the originator of this particular phrase. Later I came to find out that the author, like many writers, drew upon a biblical reference to describe a modern day situation. Once you become familiar with a phrase you hear it pop up in more conversations—for example:

> I really don't like the new taxes, but what can I do. All that is controlled by *the powers that be.*

> Actually the committee came up with several very good suggestions. Now they have to submit them to *the powers that be.*

I think it is an interesting reference to those in authority in calling them "the powers that be." It was a reference that St. Paul chose in addressing the Romans.

BIBLE USE: As one might imagine, there were many questions and issues to be resolved in the early days of the church. One of the most critical to many of the early believers was whether or not they should submit to following the civil laws issued and enforced by governments. St. Paul answered this very clearly when he said:

Powers That Be

Let every soul be subject to the governing authorities. For there is no authority except from God, and the *authorities that exist* are appointed by God.

"The authorities that exist" is synonymous with "the powers that be." While we are on the earth we must live within the community's and the country's laws and regulations, or there would be utter chaos. The challenge for people of faith is to fulfill the requirements of society while keeping the commandments of our God. At times conscientious objection or civil disobedience may be called for. But in the best of societies most laws parallel Judaeo-Christian values. We are on the earth, but we are of God, our Father.

Race Is Not Always to the Swift

(Ecclesiastes 9:11)

EVERYDAY USE: "The race is not always to the swift." That certainly came as good news to me, I can tell you. I was not only slow as a child, I was sssssllllooowww. I once came in eleventh in a ten-man race! Really, I did! The guy who starts the race, you know, the one with the starter gun, he crossed the finish line before I did. I did manage to cross the finish line ahead of some other children one time. The only problem was that I was running a hundred yard dash and they were finishing a two mile run.

The important thing is that I stayed with it. I persevered, made a lot of good friends, and had a lot of fun. When we say that the race is not always to the swift, we are saying that on any given day, anyone can win.

The home team is really an underdog today. But hey, *the race is not always to the swift.*

Justine worked hard, practiced often, and won the big race. So as you can see, *the race is not always to the swift.*

BIBLE USE: The Bible finds many ways to offer us valuable lessons for our everyday life as well as our spiritual life. Ecclesiastes offers us many passages that enjoin us to live life to the fullest, celebrating all the seasons of life in their proper turn. In the passage which gives us this familiar Bible phrase, the author is telling people that we all have equal opportunity in life. Listen to his words:

> I returned and saw under the sun
> That *the race is not to the swift*,
> Nor the battle to the strong,
> Nor bread to the wise,
> Nor riches to men of understanding,
> Nor favor to men of skill;
> But time and chance happen to them all.

Again and again the Bible tells us that we are all equal in God's sight. It is important that you do your best in life, whether or not your best brings you medals and riches. For ultimately we will not be judged by what we have accomplished, but how hard we have tried. Do your best, give your best, and remember: *the race is not always to the swift.*

SALT OF THE EARTH

(Matthew 5:13)

EVERYDAY USE: This phrase is used when speaking of a person or group of persons who hold great value. It is derived from the value salt held in ancient times. Salt has been a food additive and preservative for centuries. Therefore, a person of value was compared to salt.

> She does so much for her family and for her community. She is truly the *salt of the earth.*

> He's steady, strong, and single-minded. *He's the salt of the earth.*

Ironically, this phrase itself has been preserved in its original use and context ever since Jesus first used it.

BIBLE USE: This familiar phrase from the Bible comes at the end of the beatitudes, one of Jesus' most endearing sermons, wherein he tells us clearly who is beautiful in God's sight. He was trying to impress on the multitudes that had gathered, the great worth they have in God's eyes. Hear again his words.

> *You are the salt of the earth;* but if the salt loses its flavor, how shall it be seasoned? It is then good for nothing but to be thrown out and trampled underfoot by men.

We hear every day that our world is slipping further and further into the darkness of violence and sin. Yet, as believers, there is much we can do to *preserve* our world. We, like the early followers to whom Jesus spoke, are *the salt of the earth* in our world today.

Skin of Your Teeth

(Job 19:20)

EVERYDAY USE: We may all be able to think of more everyday uses of this phrase than we would like. It describes the very uncomfortable feeling of just barely getting by. Actually, the teeth have no skin, so what it meant is that we escaped from a situation by a narrow margin.

Do any of these sentences sound familiar to you?

I passed that test *by the skin of my teeth.*

You were running late, but I see you've made it, *by the skin of your teeth.*

Well, you won this game, but only *by the skin of your teeth.*

If you are like me, you've used this phrase many times. Did you know you were expressing a thought that was nearly 3,600 years old. Let's look at the origin of this thought in the Bible.

BIBLE USE: This thought was originally expressed by Job, a God-fearing man who lived in a land called Uz.

My bones cling to my skin and to my flesh, and I have escaped *by the skin of my teeth.*

Every time I heard this phrase after I came to

94

know the circumstances in which it was first used, I thanked God that my life is different than Job's. I also thank God for Job's example and I pray for the courage I need to stand by my faith.

Speak for Yourself

(Acts 26:1)

EVERYDAY USE: This is an easy expression to relate to, given the many cases in which one hears it used. It's a fairly simple phrase that carries some good advice with it!

Once, when our eighth grade coach asked who would stay after basketball practice to help clean up the gym, I quickly answered that my best friend Tom and I would gladly stay. Tom's quick reply to me was: *"Speak for yourself."*

> Maybe there has been a time in your life when you felt comfortable speaking on behalf of others, only to hear them say: *"Speak for yourself."*

In modern use the phrase might be better identified with a phrase often used in courts of law. *"What do you have to say for yourself?"* might actually be a phrase closer in meaning to the original use of *speak for yourself.*

BIBLE USE: To find the original context of this familiar phrase we must turn to the book of Acts. The circumstance surrounding this phrase was that some of the people wanted St. Paul to be punished and put to death for the message he was preaching. They appealed to King Agrippa, bringing many false charges against Paul. The king explained that it was not his practice to send a man to destruction until that man had a chance

96

to face his accusers and answer all the charges brought against him. That is what he says in Acts 26:1:

> Then Agrippa said to Paul, "You are permitted to *speak for yourself.*"

Though we may often tease one another, when we disagree, by saying "*Speak for yourself,*" we must remember what a great and joyous blessing we have to be able to speak freely about ourselves, our country, and our love of God. A lot of great people, in old and modern times, suffered a great deal to make sure we'd have the right to *speak for ourselves.*

SPIRIT IS WILLING

(Matthew 26:40-41)

EVERYDAY USE: This phrase is most often used to describe why certain efforts at reforming oneself fall short of the mark.

> I was trying to quit smoking, but you know how it is—*the spirit is willing but the flesh is weak.*

> I thought I could walk away from the whole situation, make a clean start of things, but I always found myself going back. *The spirit is willing but the flesh is weak.*

In our everyday lives many thoughts of improving ourselves flow through our minds. You may want to become stronger, study harder, or conduct yourself with more discipline. I know I've found myself with all those goals and more. Yet I am often disappointed at the results of my efforts. How much more disappointed must the original prophets and apostles have been to know that their efforts fell short of their goal.

BIBLE USE: This phrase comes to us from the Bible during Jesus' prayers in the garden the night before he suffered on the cross. He asked his disciples to stay awake and pray with him. The apostles had every intention of staying awake with Jesus, as any of us would want to do. But when Jesus came to check on his disciples, he found them asleep.

Then he came to the disciples and found them sleeping, and said to Peter, "What? Could you not watch with me one hour? Watch and pray, lest you enter into temptation. *The spirit is willing but the flesh is weak.*"

Jesus would not want us to downgrade ourselves for the failings we may experience in our struggle to overcome our weakness. Remember to take heart as you try to improve yourself and remember to call on the heart of Jesus to help you. Jesus' way overcomes all, even the weakness of our flesh.

Strain on a Gnat And Swallow a Camel

(Matthew 23:23-24)

EVERYDAY USE: This phrase suggests that a person can pay too much attention to small details and not enough attention to the larger, more important ones. It may not be one of the most frequently heard phrases from the Bible, but it is one of the more colorful ones.

Here are a few ways in which people use the phrase in today's language:

> He spent all that time worrying about how the car looked and not much time on how it ran. The boy would strain on a *gnat and swallow a camel.*

> If they weren't so concerned with finding out what everybody else thought, they might be able to develop some opinions of their own. But they don't. They worry over small unimportant details, like *straining on a gnat and swallowing a camel.*

BIBLE USE: A mark of a good teacher is the ability to take a concept and express it in terms that most people can understand. Jesus was a great teacher because he taught the lessons of God with authority and vivid imagery.

The imagery of straining to swallow something as

small as a gnat, and then swallowing a whole camel with no problem, brings home the point that too often we can fret over the wrong things. In this Bible passage Jesus is telling the Pharisees that they concentrate on the wrong parts of God's teachings. Hear the passage right before the one which contains our phrase:

Woe to you, scribes and Pharisees, hypocrites! For you pay tithe of mint and anise and cumin, and have neglected the weightier matters of the law: justice and mercy and faith. These you ought to have done, without leaving the others undone. Blind guides, who *strain out a gnat and swallow a camel.*

When we hear this phrase in our daily lives it will help to remind us that we might be concentrating our efforts in the wrong area.

Sweat Blood

(Luke 22:41-44)

EVERYDAY USE: The moisture released from our bodies in the form of sweat is the body's way of trying to cool down our skin temperature. Excessive strain on the body due to physical labor or mental stress actually creates a "fever" that must be cooled. If you've ever seen someone working up a "good sweat," I'm sure you'll agree that it's amazing how much water some bodies will expel in an effort to cool down. I have seen some people working so hard it actually looks as though they've jumped in a swimming pool. When stress exceeds reasonable limits, we often say that one is "sweating blood" because they're under so much strain.

> The election results were so close that both candidates were *sweating blood.*

> He pushed them to work so hard, it's a wonder they weren't *sweating blood* by the time they finished.

> If we turn to the gospel of Luke, we'll learn more of the original circumstances surrounding this phrase.

BIBLE USE: Like so much of our everyday language, the phrase "sweating blood" is a figurative one. However, the original case of a person sweating blood was anything but figurative. It was real. It happened to Jesus as he prayed in the garden of Gethsemane the night before his death.

And he was withdrawn from them about a stone's throw, and he knelt down and prayed, saying "Father, if it is your will, take this cup away from me; nevertheless not my will, but yours, be done." Then an angel appeared to him from heaven, strengthening him. And being in agony, he prayed more earnestly. Then *his sweat became like great drops of blood falling down to the ground.*

Whenever we find ourselves under some terrible stress, a stress that builds inside of us until we feel we will burst, we should call upon God to help us endure our struggles. God brings comfort as no earthly source can for, in Jesus, God knows what it is to suffer. Therefore he will quickly come to our aid when we call to him from the depths of our hearts.

THORN IN YOUR SIDE

(2 Corinthians 12:7)

EVERYDAY USE: Actually a thorn anywhere in your flesh would be quite bothersome, wouldn't it? The original phrasing of this idiom was "a thorn in your flesh" and is largely taken to mean an annoyance of any kind. Draw a mental picture of a thorn protruding from your skin in such an area that, no matter how you moved, it put pressure on the thorn and shot pain through your body. That is how some people choose to describe other people or situations.

> Here she comes again, with that same look on her face. I'm telling you, she's a *thorn in my side.*"

> These meetings every afternoon are becoming quite a *thorn in my side.*

It would serve us well to take a moment and remember that this figure of speech draws its origin from an actual event.

BIBLE USE: The reason this phrase is able to depict a bothersome situation in such a graphic way is that it would be extremely uncomfortable to have a thorn stuck in one's flesh. That is the phrase used by St. Paul to describe his own suffering, which gave rise to this everyday expression.

And lest I should be exalted above measure by the abundance of the revelations, a *thorn in the flesh* was given to me, a messenger of Satan to buffet me, lest I be exalted above measure.

St. Paul is explaining how he was reminded of his own human frailty by the presence of a thorn in his side (some ailment or temptation, which he never names). He writes this to the Corinthians at a time when he was receiving many revelations from God. As you might imagine, it could easily make most people swell with pride to realize that God was speaking through them. St. Paul was very aware of the need for humility. Notice how he declares that the thorn was *given* to him—as though it were a present. The one trait that all the saints share in common is that they looked positively on any situation that brought them closer to God. That meant sorrowful occasions as well as joyful ones. If we can adopt their outlook, then life will deliver far fewer thorns into our flesh.

WAY OF ALL FLESH

(1 Kings 2:1-2)

EVERYDAY USE: This is a somber, sad phrase for those who do not have the gift of faith. It is another way of saying that all people meet with their earthly end at some point or another.

Alas, last Saturday Robert went the *way of all flesh*, passing from us in his sleep.

Our stay in our earthly home is but a temporary one. One thing is certain—all of us, one day, will travel the *way of all flesh*. Blessed are those who travel that journey marked with the sign of faith.

Like many of the statements in the Bible, the deeper meaning of this phrase can best be understood from a faith perspective. Let us look at it in its biblical context.

BIBLE USE: This phrase is taken from the book of 1 Kings. The words are those of King David speaking to his son Solomon.

Now the days of David drew near that he should die, and he charged Solomon his son, saying, "I go the *way of all the earth*; be strong, therefore, and prove yourself a man."

When King David said "the way of all the earth," he meant that everything of the earth must eventually meet with death. Certainly there is sorrow and a sense of loss when one who is close to us goes on ahead of us. However, everything that faith has taught us reveals that if we live by God's commandments we will have eternal happiness and peace, never again to be separated from those we love, and those who love us.

We must remember that the *way of all flesh* is not the way God has designed for us. Our flesh, our bodies, were only meant to be temporary temples to house an eternal spirit. With a happy heart and joyous anticipation we must remember that we are in the world, but not of it. What the rest of the world regards with sorrow, we should hold in joy. When our bodies go the way of all flesh, our spirits will find an eternal abode in and with God.

WEIGHED IN THE BALANCE

(Daniel 5:27-28)

EVERYDAY USE: For balance to be achieved, what is on one side must be equal to that on the opposite side. We balance ourselves on seesaws by having equal amounts of weight on either end. We balance ourselves on bicycles by holding our center of gravity between the force of our wheels.

To "weigh" something can have several meanings. Obviously the first meaning is to find out the actual weight of an object by placing it on a scale. Another meaning of "weigh" is to consider the advantages or disadvantages of something—the "pros and cons" as they are often called.

> His recent actions were *weighed in the balance* of his overall accomplishments, and he was given a break.

> Her personality was *weighed in the balance* along with her inexperience, and she was given the job. Many people feel she'll do an extremely effective job in her new position.

The original Bible phrase did not have such a favorable meaning for the person whom it described.

BIBLE USE: Earlier we discussed the phrase, "your days are numbered" from the book of Daniel. "Weighed in the balance" is another phrase adapted into modern use from the same chapter of Daniel.

As you recall, Daniel was called upon to interpret the handwriting that appeared on King Belshazzar's wall during a huge feast he was throwing for a thousand of his lords. The interpretation of the words took three parts, the first of which was the phrase "your days are numbered." The second interpretation said:

> You have been *weighed in the balances and found wanting.* Your kingdom has been divided, and given to the Medes and the Persians.

During our lives we are constantly called upon to weigh our actions against their cost. We must achieve a balance in our lives that allows us to serve the commandments of God while we fulfill our earthly duties. When you feel off balance about something it probably means you don't feel it is the right thing to do.